Percy

the
Puzzle Piece

by
Mike Bennett

Leavitt Peak Press

ISBN: 978-1-969865-23-7 (sc)
ISBN: 978-1-969865-24-4 (e)

Rev. date: 10/13/2025

Dedication

This book is dedicated to my daughter, who inspired the story with her sweet and thoughtful actions. I truly believe God has gifted you with hospitality, and I pray that you will never lose sight of that precious gift and that you will continue to grow in His grace and use your gift for His glory.

Acknowledgments

I would like to acknowledge my wife and my friends for helping me in the process of writing this story. Without you, "Percy" would not have truly come to life. Thank you, Laura, Melanie, and Lanette.

Kristen sat on her bed with the soft, purple comforter wrapped around her. Once in a while, a bright flash of lightning would light up her room. She looked outside at the rain clouds. *That's how I feel, she thought, all dark and stormy.* A few tears slid down her cheeks, like the raindrops on her window. *I just don't fit in at this new school. I have trouble catching the ball at recess, and in choir I feel like a piano string that is out of tune. Maybe this isn't the right school for me, and I won't ever fit in here.*

The next day when Kristen came home, she lay down on the living room carpet in front of the warm fireplace, putting a puzzle together. She thought about her school and how nice it would be to fit in. More tears slid down her cheeks.

As she reached for another piece of her puzzle, it jumped up and said, "Hi! My name is Percy. I want to find where I fit into this puzzle!" With that, he began to run around the puzzle looking for his spot.

5

"This is where I go!" he shouted as he tried to fit into an empty spot in the puzzle. But no matter how long he stayed there, Percy knew he wouldn't fit, so he got up and kept searching.

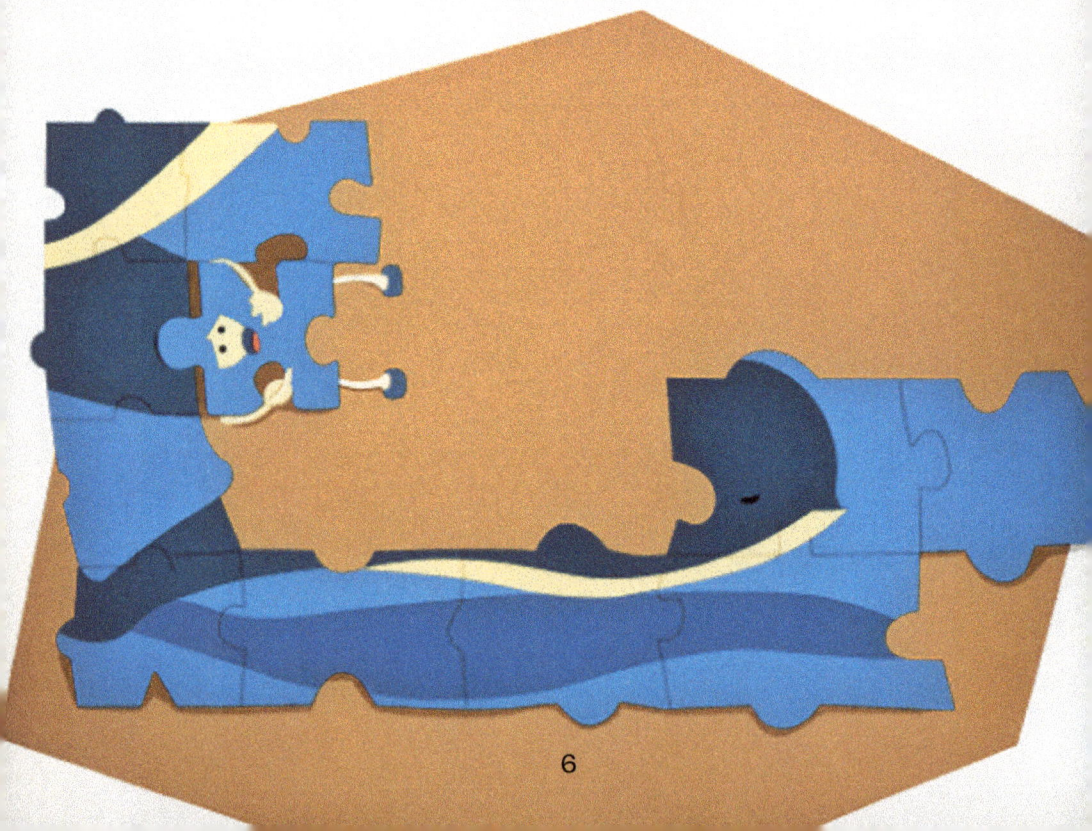

He ran to the edge of the puzzle. "Oh, this is where I go," he said.

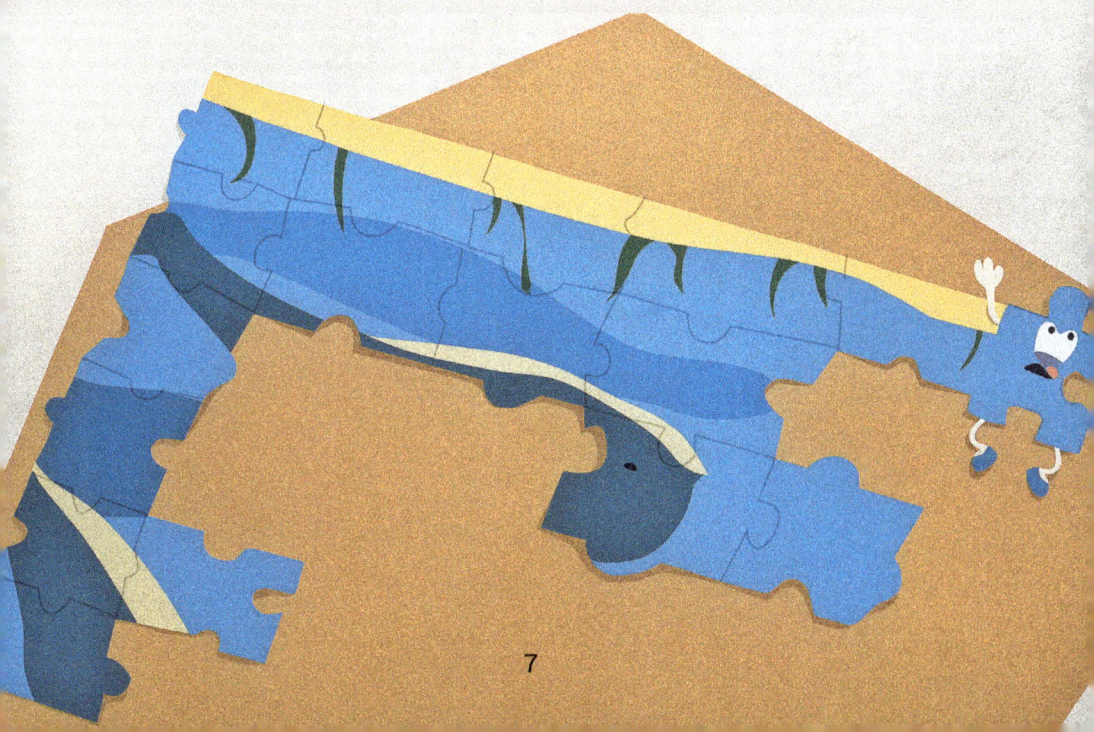

Next he chose a spot that was close to the right color.

"Look!" he exclaimed, "my colors match! This has to be where I fit."

"Uh oh." He gasped as he tried to twist and turn. Finally he popped out of the space. "Whew! I almost got stuck." Percy breathed. "And I definitely didn't fit there!"

Kristen sat with her mouth open, her eyes wide. All she could do was watch as Percy ran back and forth across the puzzle, trying different places to see if he fit. "This must be where I go!" he shouted again. "Hmm, that didn't work, but this looks like where I go." He laughed as he tried another spot.

Kristen smiled at Percy. She thought, No matter how many times he has to get up, he just keeps trying because he knows he fits this picture somewhere. Finally, Percy chose a spot that was the same color and almost the right shape, but his tabs didn't quite fit the other pieces. Instead of giving up, he excitedly told her, "I'm getting close!" He tried another spot, then another and another. Finally, with what Kristen thought must have been his hundredth try, Percy plopped himself right into the perfect spot!

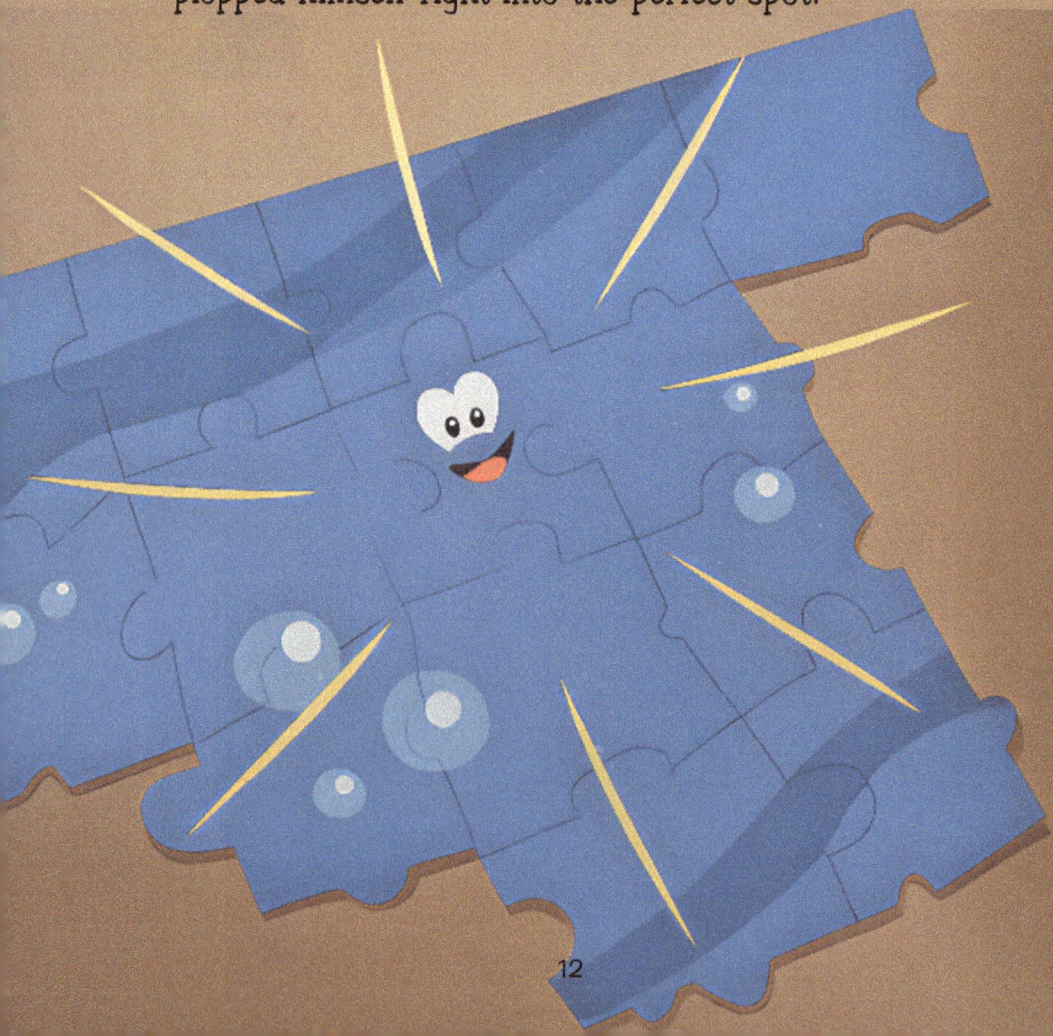

"I fit" he shouted, as Kristen clapped her hands and cheered.

"Kristen... Kristen," called her mother. Slowly Kristen opened her eyes and realized she had been napping!

Percy was a funny dream that reminded her of some-thing Daddy had told her one day when he was mowing the lawn. Kristen noticed he looked very hot and tired, so she took him a big glass of cold water. After drinking the water, he said, "You know, Kristen, Jesus gives everyone a gift so they can help Him with His work. You care so much if other people are comfortable that I think Jesus has given you a special gift."

Kristen's eyes sparkled, and she jumped up and down with excitement. "What gift, Daddy?"

"I think Jesus has given you the gift to help people," he said. "Someday you are going to find just the right place to fit in."

That's it! she thought. Maybe I can't catch very well, but I can help if someone falls down and gets hurt or maybe help the smaller children with their games. I do have trouble with choir, but maybe the teacher will let me help pass out the song sheets or turn pages for the piano player.

As she knelt by her bed that night, Kristen asked Jesus to help her find where she would fit at school.

The next day, she remembered Percy and looked for ways to help others. She volunteered to set up chairs for choir and pass the song sheets around. At recess she helped a little girl who had fallen down...

And brought cold water out for the boys.

And during spelling she was able to help another girl in her class study for their test, and they both did very well!

By the time school got out for the day, Kristen had made several new friends and she felt so happy that she sang all the way home. It seemed like her troubles were over. Just like Percy, she had found where she fit in!

www.ingramcontent.com/pod-product-compliance
Lightning Source LLC
Chambersburg PA
CBHW052126030426
42335CB00025B/3132